Quantity and Quality of Stormwater Collected from Selected Stormwater Outfalls at Industrial Sites, Fort Gordon, Georgia, 2012

By Doug D. Nagle

Prepared in cooperation with the U.S. Department of the Army Environmental and Natural Resources Management Office of the U.S. Army Signal Center and Fort Gordon

Open-File Report 2013–1140

U.S. Department of the Interior
U.S. Geological Survey

U.S. Department of the Interior
SALLY JEWELL, Secretary

U.S. Geological Survey
Suzette M. Kimball, Acting Director

U.S. Geological Survey, Reston, Virginia: 2013

For more information on the USGS—the Federal source for science about the Earth, its natural and living resources, natural hazards, and the environment, visit http://www.usgs.gov or call 1–888–ASK–USGS.

For an overview of USGS information products, including maps, imagery, and publications,
visit http://www.usgs.gov/pubprod

To order this and other USGS information products, visit http://store.usgs.gov

Suggested citation:
Nagle, D.D., 2013, Quantity and quality of stormwater collected from selected stormwater outfalls at industrial sites, Fort Gordon, Georgia, 2012: U.S. Geological Survey Open-File Report 2013–1140, 24 p., http://pubs.usgs.gov/of/2013/1140/.

Contents

Figures

Tables

Conversion Factors and Datums

Multiply	By	To obtain
Length		
inch (in.)	2.54	centimeter (cm)
inch (in.)	25.4	millimeters (mm)
foot (ft)	0.3048	meter (m)
mile (mi)	1.609	kilometer (km)
Flow rate		
cubic foot per second (ft^3/s)	0.0283	cubic meter per second (m^3/s)

Horizontal coordinate information is referenced to the North American Datum of 1983 (NAD 83).

Abbreviations

GaDNR   Georgia Department of Natural Resources

H&C   heating and cooling

LRL   laboratory reporting limit

mg/L   milligram per liter

µg/L   microgram per liter

MDL   method detection level

NPDES   National Pollutant Discharge Elimination System

NWIS   National Water Information System

NWQL   National Water Quality Laboratory

PAH   polycyclic aromatic hydrocarbon

QA   quality assurance

QC   quality control

SDI-12   serial data interface at 12 baud

USEPA   U.S. Environmental Protection Agency

USGS   U.S. Geological Survey

SWP3   Stormwater Pollution Prevention Plan

Quantity and Quality of Stormwater Collected from Selected Stormwater Outfalls at Industrial Sites, Fort Gordon, Georgia, 2012

By Doug D. Nagle

Abstract

An assessment of the quantity and quality of stormwater runoff associated with industrial activities at Fort Gordon was conducted from January through August 2012. The assessment was provided to satisfy the requirements from a general permit that authorizes the discharge of stormwater under the National Pollutant Discharge Elimination System from a site associated with industrial activities. The stormwater quantity refers to the runoff discharge at the point and time of the runoff sampling. The study was conducted by the U.S. Geological Survey, in cooperation with the U.S. Department of the Army Environmental and Natural Resources Management Office of the U.S. Army Signal Center and Fort Gordon.

Stormwater runoff samples were collected from five stations at four industrial sites, including two landfills (SWR11–1 and SWR11–2) and three heating and cooling sites, SWR11–3, SWR11–4, and SWR11–5. The assessment included the collection of physical properties, such as water temperature, specific conductance, dissolved oxygen, and pH; the detection of suspended materials (total suspended solids, total fixed solids, and total volatile solids), nutrients and organic compounds, and major and trace inorganic compounds (metals); and for the three heating and cooling sites, the detection of volatile and semivolatile organic compounds.

Landfill site SWR11–2 had the greatest total suspended solid concentration (214 milligrams per liter) of all sites and exceeded the daily maximum effluent limit for landfills. Heating and cooling site SWR11–3 had the greatest total suspended solid concentration (169 milligrams per liter), total fixed solids (101 milligrams per liter), and total volatile solids (68 milligrams per liter) when compared to the three heating and cooling sites. Total nitrogen and phosphorus concentrations were 1.02 and 0.09, and 1.74 and 0.21 milligrams per liter, respectively, at landfill sites SWR11–1 and SWR11–2. At heating and cooling sites, total nitrogen and phosphorus concentrations ranged from 0.53 to 1.08 milligrams per liter and 0.07 to 0.1 milligram per liter, respectively, with the highest concentrations measured at site SWR11–3. Additionally, oil and grease concentrations at all sites were compared to applicable benchmark standards; no sample concentrations exceeded these standards.

The estimated dissolved concentrations of cadmium, lead, nickel, zinc, mercury, and silver, and the total recoverable concentrations of arsenic and selenium were compared to applicable benchmark levels and to acute and chronic effect aquatic-life criteria for further screening purposes. The estimated dissolved zinc concentration (105 micrograms per liter) at site SWR11–3 was the only constituent to exceed a benchmark standard (40 micrograms per liter). Estimated dissolved zinc concentrations at sites SWR11–4 and SWR11–5 exceeded acute and chronic effect aquatic-life criteria. Estimated dissolved concentrations of lead exceeded the chronic effect aquatic-life criteria at all sites and exceeded the acute effect criteria at site SWR11–3. Acute and chronic effect aquatic-life criteria for dissolved cadmium were exceeded at site SWR11–3.

Samples from sites SWR11–3, SWR11–4, and SWR11–5 were analyzed for 83 volatile and semivolatile organic compounds. Eight polycyclic aromatic hydrocarbon compounds, benzo[a]pyrene, benzo[b]fluoranthene, benzo[ghi] perylene, benzo[k]fluoranthene, chrysene, indeno[1,2,3-cd] pyrene, phenanthrene, and pyrene, were detected at all three sites. Of the 86 volatile and semivolatile organic compounds that were analyzed in stormwater samples from heating and cooling sites, 15 (18 percent) were detected at site SWR11–3, 12 (14 percent) were detected at site SWR11–4, and 17 (20 percent) were detected at site SWR11–5.

Introduction

Fort Gordon is a U.S. Department of the Army facility located in east-central Georgia, approximately 10 miles (mi) outside of Augusta, Georgia (fig. 1). Five outfalls on four industrial sites located within the Fort Gordon area were sampled to determine the water quantity and quality of the runoff from January through August 2012 (fig. 1). The quantity of the runoff refers to the discharge measured at the time and location of the sample. The U.S. Department of the

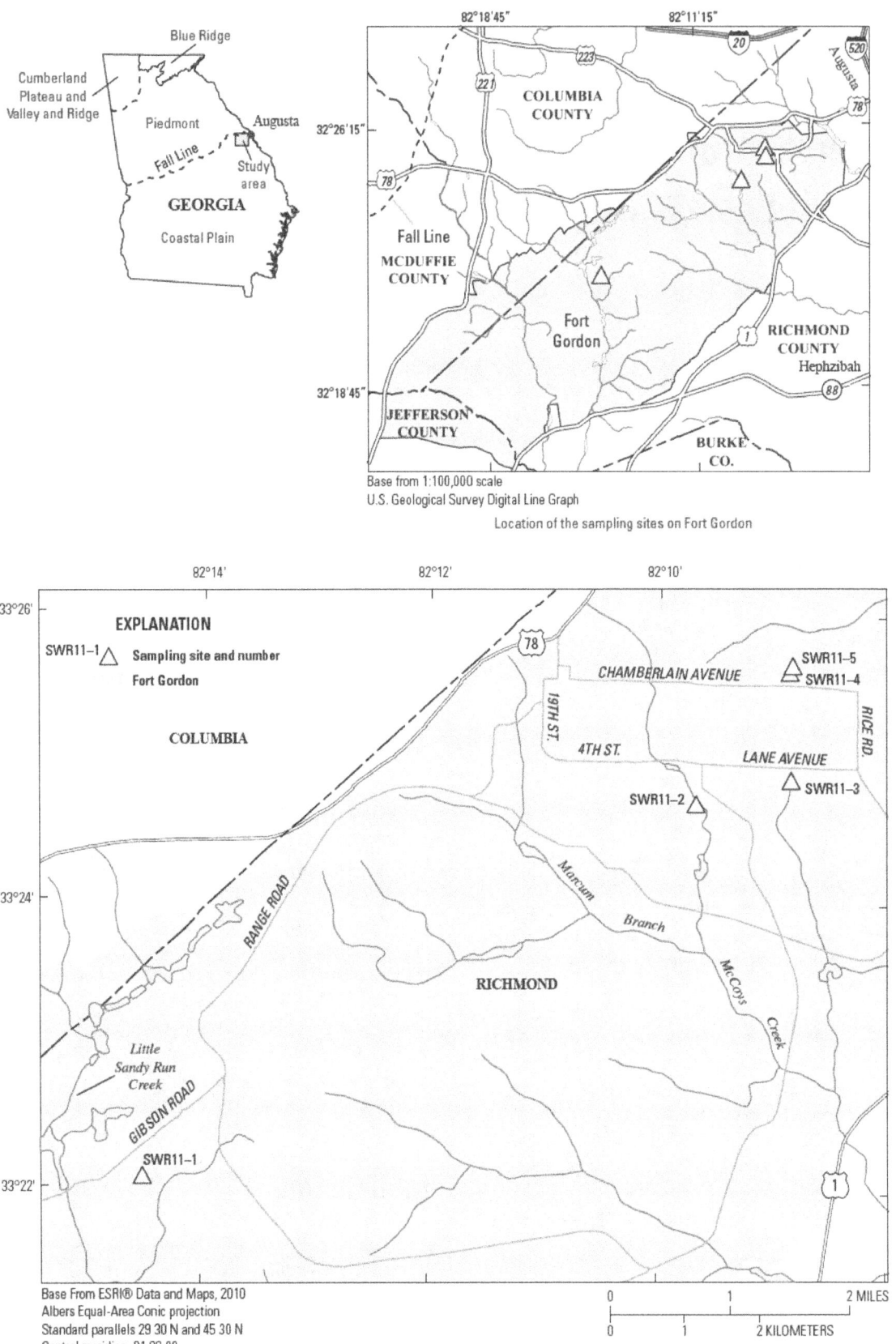

Figure 1.   Stormwater industrial sites sampled in 2012, Fort Gordon, Georgia.

Army uses water-quality information from stormwater samples to support development of a Stormwater Pollution Prevention Plan (SWP3) as required by the State of Georgia Department of Natural Resources (GaDNR) Environmental Protection Division under a general permit to discharge stormwater associated with industrial activities (Georgia Department of Natural Resources, 2012a). An effective SWP3 ensures that natural resource conservation measures and Army activities are consistent with National Pollutant Discharge Elimination System (NPDES) Federal and State requirements to manage such installations. Under the general permit, numeric effluent limitations have been established for industrial facilities through the NPDES (Georgia Department of Natural Resources, 2012a). Numeric limitations are assigned for landfills, but no numeric limitations are listed for heating and cooling sites.

Purpose and Scope

The purpose of this report is to describe the quantity and quality of stormwater collected from January through August 2012 by the U.S. Geological Survey (USGS) at selected stormwater outfall locations associated with industrial activities at Fort Gordon, Georgia. The U.S. Army at Fort Gordon was provided water-quality data from a single storm event at the selected outfalls. The stormwater data are needed to support the SWP3 and be in compliance with the general permit that allows discharges from sites associated with industrial activities (Georgia Department of Natural Resources, 2006 and 2012a). The sampling targeted stormwater runoff at five outfall locations from four sites (fig. 2). Two outfalls were sampled from a single industrial site.

Description of the Study Area

Fort Gordon is a U.S. Army facility located in east-central Georgia, approximately 10 mi southwest of Augusta, Georgia (fig. 1). Fort Gordon lies in the northern part of the Coastal Plain Physiographic Province and south of the Fall Line. Surficial soil and sediments are characterized by the unconsolidated sands, indurated sands and semiconsolidated sandstones, and layers of clay that include kaolinite (Gregory and others, 2001).

The five outfall locations had an individual station name and number assigned by the USGS to allow data entry and archival into the National Water Information System (NWIS) database (fig. 2, table 1). For this study, two of the five outfall locations scheduled for sampling were classified as landfill sites (site SWR11–1, Gibson Road landfill; and site SWR11–2, 17th Street landfill) (table 1, fig. 2). The remaining three outfall locations were classified as heating and cooling (H&C) plants (site SWR11–3, H&C plant # 310; and sites SWR11–4

and SWR11–5, H&C plant # 25910) (table 1, fig. 2). Impervious surface covers much of the drainage area at the H&C plants. Because of this site characteristic, only minor infiltration occurs during storm events and sufficient discharge at the associated stormwater outfall is available for sampling during most storm events. Conversely, the landfill areas have negligible impervious cover. This allows stormwater to infiltrate and requires much greater rainfall amounts before sufficient discharge at the associated stormwater outfall is available for sampling. Furthermore, runoff at the landfill sites must first fill a retention (SWR11–1) or detention (SWR11–2) pond before the discharge can be sampled and measured at the outfall location (fig. 3).

Methods

All samples were collected and processed using standard USGS and GaDNR field procedures (U.S. Geological Survey, variously dated; Georgia Department of Natural Resources, 2012a). The stormwater samples were collected as grab samples during the first 30 minutes of storm runoff at all five outfalls. Criteria for sampling required that each storm event produce at least 0.1 inch (in.) of rain 72 hours after the last measurable (more than 0.1 in.) rain event (Georgia Department of Natural Resources, 2012a). During each runoff event, automatic samplers were prepared to collect water samples at the outfall in pre-cleaned, acid-rinsed plastic containers. The samplers were automated to collect samples and measure discharge based on the preprogrammed settings. If the samplers did not automatically sample, they were manually operated to collect the sample and the discharge. Finally, if the flow depth was not sufficient to allow the automatic sampler to collect the samples, the samples were collected manually and the discharge was computed indirectly. It should be noted that a streamflow measurement is no longer required according to the latest stormwater permit issued by the State of Georgia (Georgia Department of Natural Resources, 2012a). However, because USGS personnel were in place before the storm events, a streamflow measurement was made and computed directly or indirectly. The individual samples were processed in the field before shipment to the laboratory. Sample processing included preparation (for example, compositing and filtering) and preservation (for example, acidification) of the final composite sample (U.S. Geological Survey, variously dated). Procedures that were followed were specific to the constituent that was analyzed. Pre-cleaned, acid-rinsed 8-liter (L) plastic churns were used as the compositing devices. For analysis of dissolved inorganic constituents, samples were filtered using 0.45-micron glass-fiber capsule filters that were conditioned with 2 L of deionized water. A summary of analytical methods for stormwater samples is listed in table 2.

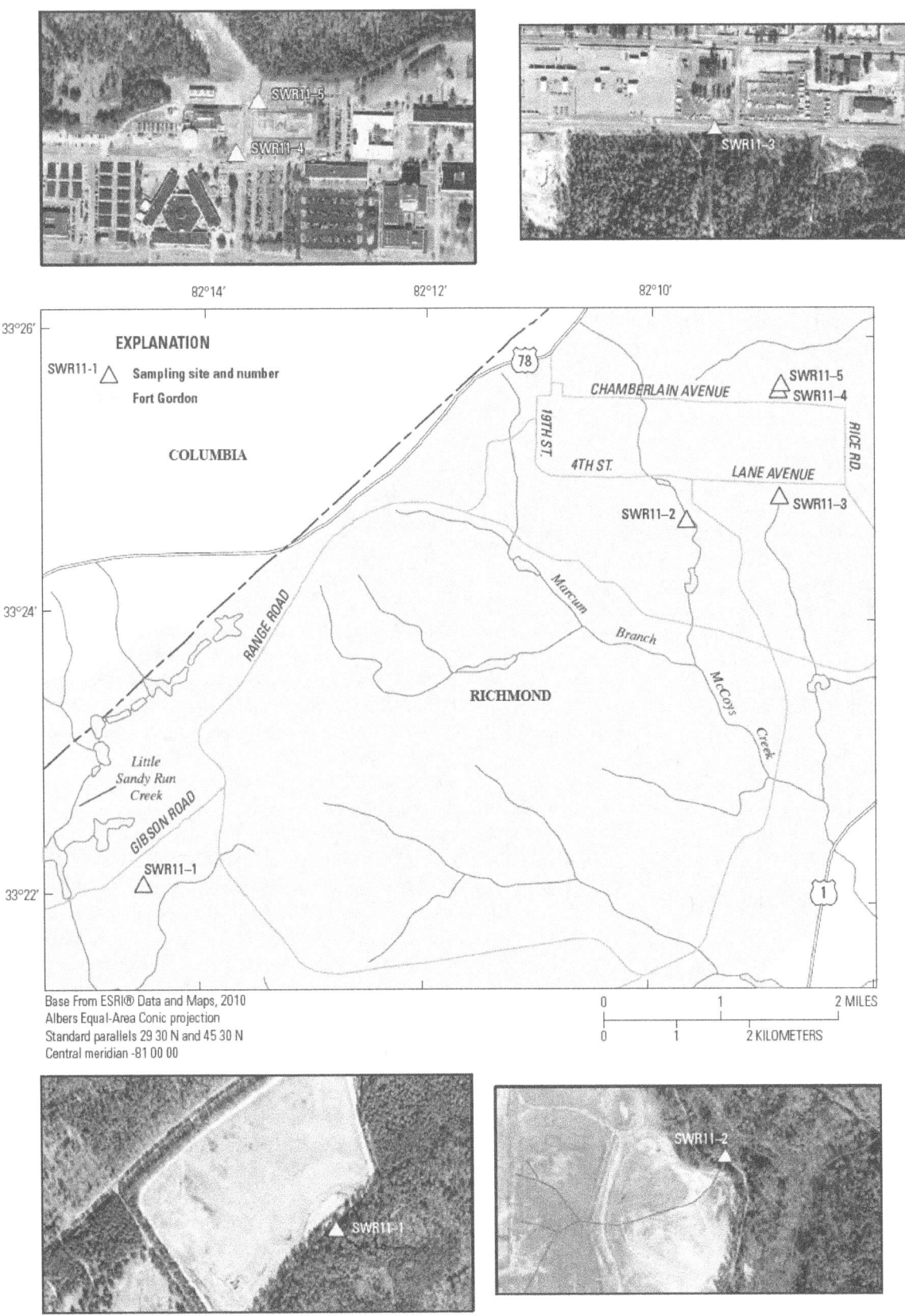

Figure 2.   Stormwater sampling sites sampled in 2012, Fort Gordon, Georgia.

Table 1.   Station identification name and number, and classification type for stations where stormwater runoff was scheduled to be sampled in 2012, Fort Gordon, Georgia.

[USGS, U.S. Geological Survey]

USGS station identification number	USGS station name (figs. 1 and 2)	Classification type	Description	Latitude	Longitude
332205082143100	SWR11–1	Landfill	Gibson Road Landfill	33° 22' 05"	82° 14' 31"
332442082094100	SWR11–2	Landfill	17th Street Landfill	33° 24' 42"	82° 09' 41"
332452082085100	SWR11–3	Heating and cooling plant	Heating and cooling plant #310	33° 24' 52"	82° 08' 51"
332538082085200	SWR11–4	Heating and cooling plant	Heating and cooling plant #25910	33° 25' 38"	82° 08' 52"
332540082085100	SWR11–5	Heating and cooling plant	Heating and cooling plant #25910	33° 25' 40"	82° 08' 51"

A

B

Figure 3.   (*A*) retention and (*B*) detention ponds at the landfill sites, Fort Gordon, Georgia.

Table 2.   Type of constituents sampled and method of analysis for stormwater samples at Fort Gordon, Georgia, 2012.

[USGS, U.S. Geological Survey; NWQL, USGS National Water Quality Laboratory; USEPA, U.S. Environmental Protection Agency; NPDES, National Pollutant Discharge Elimination System]

Constituent type	Laboratory schedule	NPDES method	Method description
Volatile organic compounds	NWQL 1307	USGS O-4127-96 (mod. USEPA 624)	[1] Purge-and-trap capillary-column gas chromatography/mass spectrometry.
Dissolved and whole water wutrients	NWQL 2352	USEPA 350.1	[2,3,4] Phosphours and Kjeldahl digestion method automated photometric finish.
Trace metals in unfiltered water	NWQL 2351	USGS I-4471-97; EPA 200.8	[4] Inductively coupled plasma-optical emission spectrometry and inductively coupled plasma-mass spectrometry.
Chemical oxygen demand		USGS I-3561-85	[3] Colorimetric, dichromate oxidation
Hardness		USEPA 200.7	[4] Inductively coupled plasma-optical emission spectrometry and inductively coupled plasma-mass spectrometry.
Total suspended solids		USGS I-3765	[2] Residue at 105 degrees Celsius, suspended, gravimetric.
Oil and grease	TestAmerica contract item number 50136	USEPA 1664	Hexane extractable material and silica gel treated hexane extractable materiol (HEM and SGT-HEM).
Semivolatile organic compounds	NWQL 1383	USGS O-3116-87	[2] Continous liquid-liquid extraction and capillary-column gas chromatography and mass spectrometry.

[1] Connor, B.F., Rose, D.L., Noriega, M.C., Murtagh, L., Abney, S.R., 1997, Methods of analysis by the U.S. Geological Survey water quality laboratories—Determination of 86 volatile organic compounds in water by gas spectrometry, including detections less than reporting limits: U.S. Geological Survey Open File Report 97–829, 78 p.

[2] Fishman, M.J, ed., 1993, Methods of analysis by the U.S. Geological Survey National Water Quality Laboratory—Determination of inorganic constituents in water and fluvial sediments: U.S. Geological Survey Open-File Report 93–125, 217 p.

[3] Fishman, M.J, and Friedman, L.C., 1989, Methods for determination of inorganic substances in water and fluvial sediments: U.S. Geological Survey Techniques of Water-Resources Investigations, book 5, chapter A1, 545 p.

[4] Patton, C.J., and Kryskalla, J.R., 2003, Methods of analysis by the U.S. Geological Survey National Water Pollution Laboratory—Evaluation of alkaline persulfate digestion as an alternative to Kjeldhal digestion for determination of total and dissolved nitrogen and phosphorus in water: U.S. Geological Survey Open-File Report 03-4174, 33 p.

Field parameters (dissolved oxygen, specific conductance, water temperature, and pH) were measured in the field using a calibrated field meter. Water samples were analyzed for constituents appropriate for each site (table 2). Samples were analyzed for nutrients, trace metals, hardness, total suspended solids, total organic carbon, chemical oxygen demand, volatile organic compounds, and semivolatile organic compounds by the USGS National Water-Quality Laboratory (NWQL) in Lakewood, Colorado (information on laboratory available at *http://nwql.usgs.gov/Public/*). Samples were analyzed for oil and grease by Test America located in Denver, Colorado (information on laboratory available at *www.testamericainc. com/home_alt.aspx*). Total organic nitrogen and ammonia and total phosphorus concentrations were determined by analyses described by Patton and Kryskalla (2003). Total ammonia concentrations were determined by EPA Method 350.1 (O'Dell, 1993). All nitrogen species concentrations are reported as milligrams per liter (mg/L) as nitrogen. All phosphorous species are reported as milligrams per liter as phosphorous. Dissolved and total trace metal concentrations were determined by inductively coupled plasma-optical emission spectrometry and inductively coupled plasma mass spectrometry (Fishman and Friedman, 1989; Fishman, 1993; Hoffman and others, 1996; Garbarino and Struzeski, 1998; Garbarino and Damrau, 2001; Garbarino and others, 2006). Total suspended solid concentrations were measured by analytical methods used to quantify concentrations of suspended organic and inorganic particles in surface waters (Fishman and Friedman, 1989). Total organic carbon was measured on whole water samples according to standard method 5310B (Standard Methods for the Examination of Water and Wastewater High-Temperature Combustion Method, 2005). Chemical oxygen demand was measured on whole water samples according to the colorimetric dichromatic oxidation HACH method (Fishman and Friedman, 1989). Volatile organic compounds were determined by using purge-and-trap capillary-column gas chromatography and mass spectrometry methods described by Connor and others (1997). Semivolatile organic compounds were measured by continuous liquid-liquid extraction and capillary-column gas chromatography and mass spectrometry analytical methods used to determine inorganic and organic constituents in water and fluvial sediments (Fishman, 1993). Oil and grease concentrations were determined according to U.S. Environmental Protection Agency (USEPA) method 1664A (U.S. Environmental Protection Agency, 1999a).

Handling censored data appropriately is necessary when laboratories report quantitative, estimated, and censored results: (1) Results above a laboratory reporting level (LRL) are reported as a quantitative value. (2) Results below the LRL and above the method detection level (MDL) are estimated (because the values are considered semiquantitative) and are reported with the remark code (E). (3) Results below the nondetection level are reported as censored data, and are reported as less than the LRL (Childress and others, 1999). For example, if the LRL for total recoverable cadmium concentration is 0.4 microgram per liter (µg/L), but was detected above the MDL of 0.2 µg/L, then an estimated value of 0.3 µg/L may be reported.

Quality Assurance and Quality Control Procedures

Quality assurance (QA) and quality control (QC) procedures maintain the integrity, accuracy, and legal defensibility of results from data collection and assessment (U.S. Environmental Protection Agency, 2009). For this study, the QA procedures included the sampling techniques, stewardship of the samples, and laboratory analyses. The QA for the sampling protocols were maintained by adherence to established procedures of the USGS and GaDNR Environmental Protection Division (U.S. Geological Survey, variously dated; Georgia Department of Natural Resources, 2012a). The stewardship of the samples refers to the preservation, hold times, and chain-of-custody of the samples. Appropriate preservation of samples (for example, placement of the samples on ice, or addition of an acid preservative) was maintained for all samples. Hold times refer to the maximum amount of time a sample can be preserved (mostly with ice) before it must be analyzed. All samples were analyzed within the appropriate hold times (National Water Quality Laboratory, 2010). The chain-of-custody ensures that the samples be accounted for from the time of sampling to the time the results are reported (U.S. Environmental Protection Agency, 2009). The chain-of-custody procedure documents who is in possession of the samples at all times, from collection to the reporting of the results. The analytical service request form and laboratory login to email served as the chain-of-custody documentation for the samples.

Water-quality data from each sampled event were reviewed for completeness, precision, bias, and transcription errors when received from the laboratory as part of the QA procedures. Collection and analysis of a QC sample was part of this study. One equipment blank was collected during this sampling period and a field blank was collected in 2011. The field blank was used to evaluate if contamination from the sampling equipment and sample processing methods affected the environmental sample concentrations. The equipment blank was used to verify that changes in cleaning procedures removed the presence of chemical oxygen demand and total organic carbon contamination identified in the field blank. Acceptable levels of contamination for field and equipment blanks are dependent on the data quality objectives of the investigation (U.S. Geological Survey, 2012). Because the data are for regulatory purposes, field blanks with detectable concentrations greater than 20 percent of the sample concentration (blank concentration to sample concentration ratio greater than 0.2) were considered to require an action (U.S. Environmental Protection Agency, 1999b; 2004). Environmental sample results with blank-to-sample concentration ratios greater than 0.2 were rejected due to potential contamination. Water-quality and rainfall data are stored in the USGS National Water Information System (NWIS) database and quality-assured water-quality data are available for retrieval on the internet at *http://waterdata.usgs.gov/sc/nwis/sw*. The USGS NWQL provides all QA/QC documentation for their analytical services on the internet at *http://nwql.usgs.gov/Public/*.

Detections were identified in the field blank for some constituents. Calcium, fluorene, and total nitrogen were all detected in the field blanks, but all at levels below the levels of the results of the environmental samples; therefore, the results of the environmental samples are considered reliable and maintained in the database (table 3). The volatile organic compound (VOC) diethyl phthalate was detected in the field blank at a level of 0.32 µg/L and present in the environmental samples SWR11–3, SWR11–4, and SWR11–5 at concentrations of less than 0.62, 0.15, and 0.31 µg/L, respectively; therefore, results for diethyl phthalate are considered unreliable for all three stations and removed from the database (table 3). Di-n-butyl phthalate was detected in the field blank at 0.89 µg/L, and concentrations in environmental samples SWR11–3, SWR11–4, and SWR11–5 were less than 2.8, estimated 0.27, and estimated 0.21 µg/L, respectively; therefore, those environmental samples also were considered unreliable and removed from the database (table 3). A phenol concentration was measured (estimated 0.16 µg/L) in the field blank and the results of the samples SWR11–3, SWR11–4, and SWR11–5 ranged from 0.06 to 0.39 µg/L; therefore, those environmental samples also were considered unreliable and removed from the database (table 3).

The greatest level of contamination in the April 2011 field blank was with chemical oxygen demand and dissolved organic carbon (table 3). After investigation of sampling preparation and field procedures, it was determined that the contamination was related to the final step of cleaning of the sampling equipment with methanol to remove trace level organic contaminants. The methanol residue contributed to the chemical oxygen demand and total organic carbon concentrations but not to other organic contaminants. Changes in cleaning procedures were implemented for the calendar year 2012 samples and a field equipment blank was conducted in June 2012 to verify the revised cleaning procedure were adequate.

Rainfall and Discharge

Each outlet location was outfitted with an ISCO 6712 automatic sampler. This sampler includes tubing that is deployed at the sampling location, a pump to bring the sample up to the sampler, and pre-cleaned containers to collect the sample (Teledyne Isco, Inc., 2012). In addition, the automatic samplers have the capability of connecting precipitation gages to a data logger using a serial data interface at 12 Baud (SDI-12) (Teledyne Isco, Inc., 2012). The SDI-12 interface can be connected to a wide range of environmental sensors, and for this study, the data logger was connected to a continuous-recording tipping-bucket precipitation gage, and to a 750-area-velocity flow module (Teledyne Isco, Inc., 2007). The continuous-recording tipping-bucket precipitation gages were deployed at four of the five sites, because one of the industrial sites had

two outfalls (H&C plant # 25910) and did not need to be equipped with a second precipitation gage (fig. 2, table 1). An equipment setup at site SWR11–5 with the precipitation gage and automatic sampler is shown in figure 4.

Nonrecording precipitation gages also were deployed during storm events near the outfall site to collect precipitation data (U.S. Environmental Protection Agency, 1992; Church and others, 1999). Data from the nonrecording precipitation gages were used to confirm the results of the recording precipitation gages, and as a backup measurement of rainfall.

Stormwater discharge, or flow, was measured by the 750-area-velocity module that uses the stage, or depth, of the stream in the culvert, the velocity of the stream in the culvert, and the culvert geometry. These parameters were recorded by the data logger in the sampler. In addition, stormwater discharge was computed by the indirect methods described by Bohdaine (1968) at all sites.

Stormwater Sampling

Stormwater was collected as grab samples as described in the GaDNR general permit for discharges associated with industrial activities (Georgia Department of Natural Resources, 2006, 2012a). At all sites, grab samples were collected manually and stormwater discharge was measured indirectly by computational methods described in the Methods section. Grab samples were collected in pre-cleaned, acid-rinsed high density polypropylene (HDLP) containers within the first 30 minutes of the runoff event (Georgia Department of Natural Resources, 2006, 2012a). All five outfalls were sampled in 2012 during rainfall events that met or exceeded the 0.1-inch criteria. Antecedent conditions varied between the two landfill sites, but all three outfalls of the H&C sites were sampled during the same rain event (table 4).

Results

The results of the multiple stormwater sample collection from the five different outfalls that were sampled during 2012 are presented in this section of the report. Results of discharge, rainfall amounts, field parameters, suspended materials, nutrients and organic compounds, major and trace inorganic compounds for landfill sites (SWR11–1 and SWR11–2), and volatile and semivolatile organic compounds from the H&C sites (SWR11–3, SWR11–4, and SWR11–5), are presented in subsequent sections. Measured concentrations are compared to appropriate standards.

Table 3.   Detected concentrations of inorganic and organic constituents in the field and equipment blanks submited for the stormwater runoff sampling, Fort Gordon, Georgia, April 13, 2011 and June 21, 2012.

[mg/L; milligram per liter; µg/L, microgram per liter; NA, not applicable; <, less than; E, estimated; Bold text indicates that the ratio of blank to environmental sample concentration is greater than 0.2.]

Constituents	Units	Field blank concentration	SWR11–1 concentration	SWR11–2 concentration	SWR11–3 concentration	SWR11–4 concentration	SWR11–5 concentration
		April 13, 2011	March 3, 2012	February 19, 2012	August 28, 2012	August 28, 2012	August 28, 2012
Calcium	mg/L	0.024	6	8.9	0.90	2.20	1.60
Fluorene	µg/L	0.0032	NA	NA	<0.34	<0.34	0.04
Total nitrogen	mg/L	0.06	1.02	1.74	1.08	0.94	0.53
Diethyl phthalate	µg/L	0.32	NA	NA	**<0.62**	**E 0.15**	**0.31**
Di-n-butyl phthalate	µg/L	0.89	NA	NA	**<2.8**	**E 0.27**	**E 0.21**
Phenol	µg/L	E 0.164	NA	NA	**0.12**	**E 0.06**	**0.39**
Chemical oxygen demand	mg/L	2,543	NA	NA	NA	NA	NA
Total organic carbon	mg/L	528	NA	NA	NA	NA	NA
Constituents	**Units**	**Equipment blank**					
		June 21, 2012	March 3, 2012	February 19, 2012	August 28, 2012	August 28, 2012	August 28, 2012
Chemical oxygen demand	mg/L	<10	20	20	60	30	20
Total organic carbon	mg/L	<0.5	9.2	8.8	16.3	20.8	7.1

Figure 4.   Automatic sampler and precipitation gage installed at selected industrial sites, Fort Gordon, Georgia.

Rainfall and Discharge

Samples were collected at the landfill sites, SWR11–2 and SWR11–1 on February 19, 2012 and March 3, 2012, respectively. On August 28, 2012 samples were collected at the H&C sites SWR11–3, SWR11–4, and SWR11–5 (table 4). Weather radars were observed to track incoming rain events, and USGS personnel were positioned at every station before the start of the rain event. Rainfall amount for the February 19, 2012 storm event was 1.0 in. and lasted for more than a period of 8.5 hours with no prior rainfall for 30 days (table 4). Rainfall amount for the March 3, 2012 storm event was a 0.1 in. and lasted for more than a period of 3.0 hours with no prior rainfall for 2 days (table 3). USGS personnel were on site a day before

this event and upon visual inspection found that the retention pond was not flowing, thus the 72-hour dry period was not applicable in this instance. On August 28, 2012, the rainfall amount was 0.1 in. at H&C site SWR11–3 and 0.3 in. at sites SWR11–4 and SWR11–5, respectively, and rainfall lasted for a period of 15 hours with no prior rainfall for 7 days (table 4). At all sites, samples were collected within the first 30 minutes of observed runoff. At all five stations, the continuously recording precipitation gages did not function correctly; therefore, the precipitation results were obtained from the nonrecording precipitation gages. Stormwater discharge at the time of sample collection ranged from 0.01 ft³/s at site SWR11–4 to 0.89 ft³/s at site SWR11–1 (table 4).

Table 4.   Streamflow and rainfall amounts, date that sample was collected, number of days from last measurable rain event, and duration of rain event, Fort Gordon, Georgia, 2012.

[USGS, U.S. Geological Survey; ft³/s, cubic feet per second; NS, not sampled; EST, eastern standard time]

USGS station name (fig. 1)	Date of sample	Number of days from previously measured storm event	Quantity of rain (inches)	Peak streamflow, instantaneous (ft³/s)	Duration of storm event (hours)
[1]SWR11–1	March 3, 2012, Hour: 09:15 EST	2	0.1	0.89	3
SWR11–2	February 19, 2012 Hour 02:15 EST	30	1	0.27	8.5
SWR11–3	August 28, 2012 Hour: 08:00 EST	7	0.1	0.5	15
SWR11–4	August 28, 2012 Hour: 10:00 EST	7	0.3	0.01	15
SWR11–5	August 28, 2012 Hour: 10:15 EST	7	0.3	0.09	15

[1] USGS personnel were on site a day before this event and upon visual inspection found that the retention pond was not flowing, thus the 72-hour dry period was not applicable in this instance.

Stormwater Sampling

Field parameters (water temperature, specific conductance, dissolved oxygen, and pH) were measured at the five stations before the samples were collected. Specific conductance values ranged from 12 to 94 microsiemens per centimeter at 25 degrees Celsius at sites SWR11–5 and SWR11–2, respectively (table 5). The pH values ranged from 4.2 to 6.9 standard units at sites SWR11–3 and SWR11–2, respectively (table 5). At landfill sites SWR11–1 and SWR11–2, pH values were 6.4 and 6.9, respectively, which are within the range of 6 to 9 published in Georgia Department of Natural Resources NPDES general permit guidance (2012a). Heating and cooling sites SW11–3 and SW11–4 had pH values that fell below 6 (4.2 and 5.7, respectively; table 4). Dissolved oxygen concentrations ranged from 6.5 to 11.2 milligrams per liter (mg/L) at sites SWR11–4 and SWR11–2, respectively (table 5).

Table 5. Field parameters detected in stormwater samples collected from selected stormwater industrial sites, Fort Gordon, Georgia, 2012.

[NS, not sampled]

Parameter	Result	Concentration unit
SW11–1		
Sample quantity	1.06	gallons
Temperature	6	degrees Celcius
Specific conductance	63	microsiemens per centimeter at 25 degrees Celcius
Dissolved oxygen	8.4	milligrams per liter
pH	6.4	standard units
SW11–2		
Sample quantity	1.06	gallons
Temperature	11	degrees Celsius
Specific conductance	94	microsiemens per centimeter at 25 degrees Celsius
Dissolved oxygen	11.2	milligrams per liter
pH	6.9	standard units
SW11–3		
Sample quantity	1.06	gallons
Temperature	26.5	degrees Celcius
Specific conductance	22	microsiemens per centimeter at 25 degrees Celcius
Dissolved oxygen	8.6	milligrams per liter
pH	4.2	standard units
SW11–4		
Sample quantity	1.06	gallons
Temperature	27.2	degrees Celcius
Specific conductance	23	microsiemens per centimeter at 25 degrees Celcius
Dissolved oxygen	6.5	milligrams per liter
pH	5.7	standard units
SW11–5		
Sample quantity	1.06	gallons
Temperature	27	degrees Celcius
Specific conductance	12	microsiemens per centimeter at 25 degrees Celcius
Dissolved oxygen	7.5	milligrams per liter
pH	6.2	standard units

Suspended material, nutrient and organic compound, and major and trace inorganic compound concentrations were determined for the stormwater samples at two landfill and three H&C sites (tables 6–10). Suspended material often is transported during storm events. At the landfill site SWR11–1, total suspended solids, total fixed solids (inorganic fraction), and total volatile solids (organic fraction) concentrations were below the LRL (less than 20 to less than 30 mg/L) during the March 2012 storm event (table 6). However, a much higher total suspended solids concentration of 214 mg/L was measured at landfill site SWR11–2 with most of the suspended solids consisting of fixed solids (176 mg/L) rather than volatile solids (38 mg/L) (table 7). The total suspended solids concentration at site SWR11–2 exceeded the maximum daily effluent limit for total suspended solids (88 mg/L) (Georgia Department of Natural Resources, 2012a).

Heating and cooling site SWR11–3 had the highest concentrations of total suspended solids (68 mg/L), total fixed solids (101 mg/L), and total volatile solids (169 mg/L) when compared to other two H&C sites, SWR11–4 and SWR11–5 (tables 8–10). There are no numeric criteria for the H&C sites.

Excessive nutrients have the potential to cause detrimental effects on the receiving water body, usually related to increased algal activity. Because total phosphorus and total nitrogen include the particulate (sediment- or organic-bound) and dissolved fractions of these nutrients, greater concentrations of these nutrients often are observed during storm events that also transport greater suspended solids. Total nitrogen concentrations were 1.02 and 1.74 mg/L at landfill sites SWR11–1 and SWR11–2, respectively (tables 6–7). Total phosphorus concentrations were 0.09 and 0.21 mg/L at landfill sites SWR11–1 and SWR11–2, respectively (tables 6–7). Total ammonia values were 0.02 mg/L at SWR11–1 (table 6) and 0.03 mg /L at SWR11–-2 (table 7), which are below the maximum daily effluent limit of 10 mg/L for landfill sites (Georgia Department of Natural Resources, 2012a). For H&C sites, SWR11–3 had the highest value of total nitrogen of 1.08 mg/L compared to 0.94 and 0.53 mg/L at sites SWR11–4 and SWR11–5, respectively (tables 8–10). Total phosphorus values were 0.1 mg/L at both sites SWR11–3 and SWR11–4 as compared to 0.07 mg/L at SWR11–5. Additionally, at the three H&C sites values for total ammonia ranged from 0.19 to 0.41 mg/L with site SWR11–3 having the highest concentration.

Biochemical oxygen demand (BOD) measures the amount of oxygen consumed by biologically-mediated decomposition of organic matter in water. The chemical oxygen demand (COD) test procedure is the amount of oxygen consumed based on the chemical decomposition of organic and inorganic contaminants, dissolved or suspended in water, and therefore, is inclusive of BOD (organic-based). Chemical oxygen demand was measured at 18 and 19.6 mg/L at landfill sites SWR11–1 and SWR11–2, respectively (tables 6–7). At these landfill sites, measured COD was well below the maximum daily effluent limit for 5-day BOD is 140 mg/L, indicating that the sites were within the permit guidelines (Georgia Department of Natural Resources, 2012a). Total organic carbon (TOC) concentrations were 9.2 and 8.8 mg/L, at landfill sites SWR11–1 and SWR11–2, respectively.

Table 6.   Suspended material, nutrients and organic compounds, and major and trace inorganic compounds detected in a single grab stormwater sample collected within the first 30 minutes of runoff from landfill site SWR11–1, Fort Gordon, Georgia, March 3, 2012.

[All units in milligrams per liter; <, less than; NR, not reported; E, estimated; N, nitrogen]

Compound	Result
Suspended material	
Total suspended solids	<30.0
Total fixed solids	<30.0
Total volatile solids	<20.0
Nutrients and organic compounds	
Chemical oxygen demand, high level	18
Total organic carbon	9.2
Ammonia, as nitrogen	0.02
Oil and grease	E 3.3
Total phosphorus	0.09
Total nitrogen (nitrate + nitrite + ammonia + organic-N)	1.02
Major and trace inorganic compounds	
Hardness	18.5
Calcium, dissolved	5.98
Barium, dissolved	12.86
Magnesium, dissolved	0.88
Arsenic, total	0.0009
Cadmium, total	<0.0004
Chromium, total	0.00061
Lead, total	0.00155
Silver, total	<0.0006
Mercury, total	<0.00007
Selenium, total	0.00013
Zinc, total	0.0111
Nickel, total	0.0011

Table 7.   Suspended material, nutrients and organic compounds, and major and trace inorganic compounds detected in a single grab stormwater sample collected within the first 30 minutes of runoff from landfill site SWR11–2, Fort Gordon, Georgia, February 19, 2012.

[All units in milligrams per liter; <, less than; NR, not reported; E, estimated; N, nitrogen]

Compound	Result
Suspended material	
Total suspended solids	214.0
Total fixed solids	176.0
Total volatile solids	38.0
Nutrients and organic compounds	
Chemical oxygen demand, high level	19.6
Total organic carbon	8.8
Ammonia, as nitrogen	0.03
Oil and grease	E 2.3
Total phosphorus	0.21
Total nitrogen (nitrate + nitrite + ammonia + organic-N)	1.74
Major and trace inorganic compounds	
Hardness	29.2
Calcium, dissolved	8.91
Barium, dissolved	35.35
Magnesium, dissolved	1.69
Arsenic, total	0.0011
Cadmium, total	<0.0004
Chromium, total	0.0062
Lead, total	0.00587
Silver, total	<0.0006
Mercury, total	0.000065
Selenium, total	0.00011
Zinc, total	0.0208
Nickel, total	0.0028

Table 8. Suspended material, nutrients and organic compounds, and major and trace inorganic compounds detected in a single grab stormwater sample collected within the first 30 minutes of runoff from heating and cooling site SWR11–3, Fort Gordon, Georgia, August 28, 2012.

[All units in milligrams per liter; <, less than; NR, not reported; E, estimated; N, nitrogen]

Compound	Result
Suspended material	
Total suspended solids	169.0
Total fixed solids	101.0
Total volatile solids	68.0
Nutrients and organic compounds	
Chemical oxygen demand, high level	60
Total organic carbon	16.3
Ammonia, as nitrogen	0.41
Oil and grease	E 3.9
Total phosphorus	0.1
Total nitrogen (nitrate + nitrite + ammonia + organic-N)	1.08
Major and trace inorganic compounds	
Hardness	2.7
Calcium, dissolved	0.868
Barium, dissolved	0.0111
Magnesium, dissolved	0.129
Arsenic, total	0.0013
Cadmium, total	0.0004
Chromium, total	0.0014
Lead, total	0.00764
Silver, total	0.0006
Mercury, total	0.000013
Selenium, total	0.000087
Zinc, total	0.107
Nickel, total	0.0013

Table 9. Suspended material, nutrients and organic compounds, and major and trace inorganic compounds detected in a single grab stormwater sample collected within the first 30 minutes of runoff from heating and cooling site SWR11–4, Fort Gordon, Georgia, August 28, 2012.

[All units in milligrams per liter; <, less than; NR, not reported; E, estimated; N, nitrogen]

Compound	Result
Suspended material	
Total suspended solids	<10.0
Total fixed solids	<15.0
Total volatile solids	<15.0
Nutrients and organic compounds	
Chemical oxygen demand, high level	30
Total organic carbon	20.8
Ammonia, as nitrogen	0.21
Oil and grease	<4.9
Total phosphorus	0.1
Total nitrogen (nitrate + nitrite + ammonia + organic-N)	0.94
Major and trace inorganic compounds	
Hardness	6.39
Calcium, dissolved	2.21
Barium, dissolved	0.129
Magnesium, dissolved	0.214
Arsenic, total	0.00028
Cadmium, total	<0.0004
Chromium, total	<0.0006
Lead, total	0.00168
Silver, total	<0.0006
Mercury, total	0.0000009
Selenium, total	0.000062
Zinc, total	0.0248
Nickel, total	<0.0011

Table 10. Suspended material, nutrients and organic compounds, and major and trace inorganic compounds detected in a single grab stormwater sample collected within the first 30 minutes of runoff from heating and cooling site SWR11–5, Fort Gordon, Georgia, August 28, 2012.

[All units in milligrams per liter; <, less than; NR, not reported; E, estimated; N, nitrogen]

Compound	Result
Suspended material	
Total suspended solids	<10
Total fixed solids	<20
Total volatile solids	20
Nutrients and organic compounds	
Chemical oxygen demand, high level	20
Total organic carbon	7.1
Ammonia, as nitrogen	0.19
Oil and grease	E 1.3
Total phosphorus	0.07
Total nitrogen (nitrate + nitrite + ammonia + organic-N)	0.53
Major and trace inorganic compounds	
Hardness	4.64
Calcium, dissolved	1.64
Barium, dissolved	0.00041
Magnesium, dissolved	0.13
Arsenic, total	0.00048
Cadmium, total	<0.0004
Chromium, total	0.0008
Lead, total	0.00132
Silver, total	<0.0006
Mercury, total	<0.000008
Selenium, total	0.000085
Zinc, total	0.0368
Nickel, total	<0.0011

Chemical oxygen demand and TOC ranged from 20 to 60 mg/L and 7.1 to 20.8 mg/L, respectively for H&C sites SWR11–3, SWR11–4, and SWR11–5. The largest COD (60 mg/L) was measured at site SWR11–3.

Oil and grease concentrations were estimated at 3.3 and 2.3 mg/L at landfill sites SWR11–1 and SWR11–2, respectively (tables 6–7). At the H&C sites, concentrations were estimated at 3.9 mg/L at site SWR11–3, less than 4.9 mg/L at site SWR11–4, and estimated 1.3 mg/L at site SWR11–5. None of these values exceeded the Benchmark Monitoring Concentration of 15 mg/L for H&C sites (Georgia Department of Natural Resources, 2012a).

Trace elements, such as lead, mercury, and arsenic, exist in surface water at very low concentrations, generally in the range of parts per billion. Even at these low levels, most trace elements can be harmful to aquatic life; however, the exact level that acutely or chronically affects aquatic life can vary with hardness. Therefore, hardness-based criteria levels are computed for certain trace elements (including cadmium, copper, lead, and zinc) for the protection of aquatic life in surface-water systems. For use in this report, the GaEPD freshwater water-quality hardness-dependent criterion for trace metals was adopted as a conservative screening limit, although it was developed for protection of aquatic life in receiving waters, not stormwater. Equations to compute these criteria for certain trace elements are provided by the USEPA (U.S. Environmental Protection Agency, 2006). Hardness ranges are used to determine benchmark values for cadmium, lead, nickel, and zinc. In order to compare concentrations of the environmental sample to the criteria values the concentration values were converted from total to dissolved (table 11). The estimated dissolved concentrations of cadmium, lead, nickel, zinc, mercury, and silver, and the total recoverable concentrations of arsenic and selenium were compared to applicable benchmark, acute and chronic effect criteria (Georgia Department of Natural Resources, 2012a, 2012b). The estimated dissolved zinc concentration (105 μg/L) at site SWR11–3 was the only constituent to exceed a benchmark standard of 40 μg/L based on the hardness-range at the site (table 11). Estimated dissolved zinc concentrations at sites SWR11–4 and SWR11–5 exceeded acute and chronic effect aquatic criteria (table 11). Estimated dissolved concentrations of lead exceeded the chronic effect criteria at all sites and exceeded the acute effect criteria at site SWR11–3. The acute and chronic effect criteria for dissolved cadmium were exceeded at site SWR11–3 (table 11).

Samples from H&C sites SWR11–3, SWR11–4, and SWR11–5 were analyzed for various semivolatile organic compounds (tables 12–14). Several compounds were detected at quantitative (above the laboratory reporting level) or estimated (semiquantitative) levels at all three sites and included eight polycyclic aromatic hydrocarbons (PAH) benzo[*a*]pyrene, benzo[*b*]fluoranthene, benzo[*ghi*] perylene, benzo[*k*]fluoranthene, chrysene, indeno[1,2,3-*cd*] pyrene, phenanthrene, and pyrene. Other semivolatile organic compounds detected at all three H&C sites included pentachlorophenol, dimethyl phthalate, and isophorone. Eight additional semivolatile organic compounds were detected at measured or estimated levels at one or two of the three sites (table 15).

Of the 83 volatile and semivolatile organic compounds that were analyzed in stormwater samples from heating and cooling sites, 15 (18 percent) were detected at site SWR11–3 (table 12), 12 (14 percent) were detected at site SWR11–4 (table 13), and 17 (20 percent) were detected at site SWR11–5 (table 14). No volatile organic compounds were detected at any of the three heating and cooling sites (table 15). Instead, the most frequently detected semivolatile organic compounds were from the polycyclic aromatic hydrocarbon (PAH) group. Of the 14 PAHs that were analyzed in the stormwater samples, between 9 and 11 (64 and 79 percent) of the compounds were detected at concentrations that ranged from E 0.03 to 0.86 μg/L (table 15). The greatest total PAH concentration (pyrene, 0.86 μg/L) was detected at site SWR11–5.

Table 11.   Acute and chronic aquatic-life criteria for hardness-dependent and nonhardness-dependent metals.

[µg/L, microgram per liter; mg/L, milligram per liter]

Station number	USGS Station name	Date of sample	Hardness (mg/L)	Acute and chronic aquatic-life Criteria (Georgia Department of Natural Resources[2]) and benchmark values (Georgia Department of Natural Resources[1]) for hardness-dependent metals							
				Dissolved cadmium (µg/L)				Dissolved Lead (µg/L)			
				Estimated concentration	Acute criteria	Chronic criteria	Bench-mark	Estimated concentration	Acute criteria	Chronic criteria	Bench-mark
332205082143100	SWR11–1	March 3, 2012	19	<0.4	0.70	0.64	0.50	1.61	9.88	0.39	14.0
332442082094100	SWR11–2	February 19, 2012	29	<0.4	1.14	0.90	0.80	5.72	16 5	0.64	23.0
332452082085100	SWR11–3	August 28, 2012	2.7	0.44	0.09	0.15	0.50	10.1	1.08	0.04	14.0
332538082085200	SWR11–4	August 28, 2012	6.4	<0.4	0.22	0.29	0.50	2.01	2 93	0.11	14.0
332540082085100	SWR11–5	August 28, 2012	4.6	<0.4	0.15	0.23	0.50	1.64	2.03	0.08	14.0

Station number	USGS Station name	Date of sample	Hardness (mg/L)	Aquatic-life acute and chronic criteria for nonhardness dependent metals in freshwater (Georgia Department of Natural Resources[2]) and benchmark values (Georgia Department of Natural Resources[2])							
				Dissolved mercury (µg/L)				Total recoverable arsenic (µg/L)			
				Estimated concentration	Acute criteria	Chronic criteria	Bench-mark	Estimated concentration	Acute criteria	Chronic criteria	Bench-mark
332205082143100	SWR11–1	March 3, 2012	19	0.01	1.4	0.77	1.40	0.93	340.00	150.00	150.0
332442082094100	SWR11–2	February 19, 2012	29	0.06	1.4	0.77	1.40	1.10	340.00	150.00	150.0
332452082085100	SWR11–3	August 28, 2012	2.7	0.01	1.4	0.77	1.40	1.30	340.00	150.00	150.0
332538082085200	SWR11–4	August 28, 2012	6.4	0.01	1.4	0.77	1.40	<0.28	340.00	150.00	150.0
332540082085100	SWR11–5	August 28, 2012	4.6	0.01	1.4	0.77	1.40	0.48	340.00	150.00	150.0

[1,2]See references cited.

Table 11.   Acute and chronic aquatic-life criteria for hardness-dependent and nonhardness-dependent metals—Continued.

[µg/L, microgram per liter; mg/L, milligram per liter; NA, not applicable]

| Station number | USGS Station name | Date of sample | Hardness (mg/L) | Acute and chronic aquatic-life criteria (Georgia Department of Natural Resources[2]) and benchmark values (Georgia Department of Natural Resources[1]) for hardness-dependent metals | | | | | | | |
| | | | | Dissolved nickel (µg/L) | | | | Dissolved zinc (µg/L) | | | |
				Estimated concentration	Acute criteria	Chronic criteria	Bench-mark	Estimated concentration	Acute criteria	Chronic criteria	Bench-mark
332205082143100	SWR11–1	March 3, 2012	19	1.1	112	57.4	150	11	28.0	28.3	40
332442082094100	SWR11–2	February 19, 2012	29	2.8	165	79.5	200	20	41.3	41.6	50
332452082085100	SWR11–3	August 28, 2012	2.7	1.3	22.0	14.5	150	105	5.49	5.5	40
332538082085200	SWR11–4	August 28, 2012	6.4	<1.1	45.7	26.8	150	24	11.4	11.5	40
332540082085100	SWR11–5	August 28, 2012	4.6	<1.1	34.9	21.3	150	36	8.69	8.8	40

| Station number | USGS Station name | Date of sample | Hardness (mg/L) | Aquatic-life acute and chronic criteria for nonhardness dependent metals in freshwater (Georgia Department of Natural Resources[2]) and benchmark values (Georgia Department of Natural Resources[2]) | | | | | | | |
| | | | | Dissolved silver (µg/L) | | | | Total recoverable selenium (µg/L) | | | |
				Estimated concentration	Acute criteria	Chronic criteria	Bench-mark	Estimated concentration	Acute criteria	Chronic criteria	Bench-mark
332205082143100	SWR11–1	March 3, 2012	19	<0.6	3.2	NA	NA	0.13	NA	5	5
332442082094100	SWR11–2	February 19, 2012	29	<0.6	3.2	NA	NA	0.11	NA	5	5
332452082085100	SWR11–3	August 28, 2012	2.7	<0.6	3.2	NA	NA	0.09	NA	5	5
332538082085200	SWR11–4	August 28, 2012	6.4	<0.6	3.2	NA	NA	0.06	NA	5	5
332540082085100	SWR11–5	August 28, 2012	4.6	<0.6	3.2	NA	NA	0.09	NA	5	5

[1,2]See references cited.

Table 12.   Volatile and semivolatile organic compounds in a single stormwater grab sample taken within the first 30 minutes of runoff from heating and cooling station SWR11–3, Fort Gordon, Georgia, August 28, 2012.

[All units in micrograms per liter; <, less than; E, estimated; NR, not reported; Bold text indicates compound detected.]

Compound	Result
1,2-Dichloroethane	<0.2
1,2-Dichloropropane	<0.1
1,4-Dichlorobenzene	<0.1
2,4,6-Trichlorophenol	<0.34
2,4-Dichlorophenol	<0.36
2,4-Dimethylphenol	<0.8
2-Methyl-4,6-dinitrophenol	<2
4-Chloro-3-methylphenol	<0.54
4-Nitrophenol	<0.52
Hexachlorobenzene	<0.3
Pentachlorophenol	**E 0.1**
1,1,1-Trichloroethane	<0.1
1,1,2-Trichloro-1,2,2-trifluoroethane	<0.1
1,1-Dichloroethane	<0.1
1,1-Dichloroethene	<0.1
1,2,4-Trichlorobenzene	<0.26
1,2-Dichlorobenzene	<0.1
1,2-Diphenylhydrazine	<0.3
1,3-Dichlorobenzene	<0.1
2,4-Dinitrophenol	<2
2,4-Dinitrotoluene	<0.56
2,6-Dinitrotoluene	<0.4
2-Chloronaphthalene	<0.24
2-Nitrophenol	<0.4
3,3'-Dichlorobenzidine	<0.42
4-Bromophenyl phenyl ether	<0.24
4-Chlorophenyl phenyl ether	<0.34
9H-Fluorene, water	<0.34
Acenaphthene	<0.28
Acenaphthylene	<0.3
Anthracene, water	<0.38
Benzene, water	<0.1
Benzo[a]anthracene	**0.04**
Benzo[a]pyrene	**0.08**
Benzo[b]fluoranthene	**E 0.15**
Benzo[ghi]perylene	**0.07**
Benzo[k]fluoranthene	**E 0.08**
Benzyl n-butyl phthalate	**E 0.6**
Bis(2-chloroethoxy)methane	<0.24
Bis(2-chloroethyl) ether	<0.3
Bis(2-chloroisopropyl) ether	<0.14

Table 12.   Volatile and semivolatile organic compounds in a single stormwater grab sample taken within the first 30 minutes of runoff from heating and cooling station SWR11–3, Fort Gordon, Georgia, August 28, 2012.—Continued

[All units in micrograms per liter; <, less than; E, estimated; NR, not reported; Bold text indicates compound detected.]

Compound	Result
Bis(2-ethylhexyl) phthalate	<7.2
Bromodichloromethane	<0.1
Chlorobenzene	<0.1
Chrysene, water	**0.12**
cis-1,2-Dichloroethene	<0.1
Dibenzo[a,h]anthracene	<0.42
Dibromochloromethane	<0.2
Dichlorodifluoromethane	<0.2
Dichloromethane	<0.2
Diethyl ether	<0.2
Diethyl phthalate	<0.62
Diisopropyl ether	<0.2
Dimethyl phthalate	**0.03**
Di-n-butyl phthalate	<2.8
Di-n-octyl phthalate	<0.6
Ethylbenzene	<0.1
Fluoranthene	**0.15**
Hexachlorobutadiene	<0.24
Hexachlorocyclopentadiene	<0.5
Hexachloroethane	<0.24
Indeno[1,2,3-cd]pyrene	**E 0.06**
Isophorone	**E 0.23**
Methyl tert-butyl ether	<0.2
Methyl tert-pentyl ether	<0.2
m-Xylene plus p-xylene	<0.2
Naphthalene	**0.03**
Nitrobenzene	<0.26
N-Nitrosodimethylamine	<0.32
N-Nitrosodi-n-propylamine	<0.4
N-Nitrosodiphenylamine	<0.48
o-Xylene	<0.1
Phenanthrene	**0.04**
Phenol	**0.12**
Pyrene	**0.12**
Styrene	<0.1
tert-Butyl ethyl ether	<0.1
Tetrachloroethene	<0.1
Tetrachloromethane	<0.2
Toluene, water	<0.1
trans-1,2-Dichloroethene	<0.1
Tribromomethane	<0.2
Trichloroethene	<0.1
Trichlorofluoromethane	<0.2
Trichloromethane	<0.1
Trihalomethanes	<0.6
Vinyl chloride	<0.2

Table 13. Volatile and semivolatile organic compounds in a single stormwater grab sample taken within the first 30 minutes of runoff from heating and cooling station SWR11–4, Fort Gordon, Georgia, August 28, 2012.

[All units in micrograms per liter; <, less than; E, estimated; NR, not reported; Bold text indicates compound detected, M; values that are detected below method detection limits but unable to be quantified.]

Compound	Result
1,2-Dichloroethane	<0.2
1,2-Dichloropropane	<0.1
1,4-Dichlorobenzene	<0.1
2,4,6-Trichlorophenol	<0.34
2,4-Dichlorophenol	<0.36
2,4-Dimethylphenol	<0.8
2-Methyl-4,6-dinitrophenol	<2
4-Chloro-3-methylphenol	<0.54
4-Nitrophenol	<0.52
Hexachlorobenzene	<0.3
Pentachlorophenol	**M**
1,1,1-Trichloroethane	<0.1
1,1,2-Trichloro-1,2,2-trifluoroethane	<0.1
1,1-Dichloroethane	<0.1
1,1-Dichloroethene	<0.1
1,2,4-Trichlorobenzene	<0.26
1,2-Dichlorobenzene	<0.1
1,2-Diphenylhydrazine	<0.3
1,3-Dichlorobenzene	<0.1
2,4-Dinitrophenol	<2
2,4-Dinitrotoluene	<0.56
2,6-Dinitrotoluene	<0.4
2-Chloronaphthalene	<0.24
2-Nitrophenol	<0.4
3,3'-Dichlorobenzidine	<0.42
4-Bromophenyl phenyl ether	<0.24
4-Chlorophenyl phenyl ether	<0.34
9H-Fluorene, water	<0.34
Acenaphthene	<0.28
Acenaphthylene	<0.3
Anthracene, water	<0.38
Benzene, water	<0.1
Benzo[a]anthracene	<0.26
Benzo[a]pyrene	**0.06**
Benzo[b]fluoranthene	**E 0.12**
Benzo[ghi]perylene	**E 0.07**
Benzo[k]fluoranthene	**E 0.05**
Benzyl n-butyl phthalate	<1.8
Bis(2-chloroethoxy)methane	<0.24
Bis(2-chloroethyl) ether	<0.3
Bis(2-chloroisopropyl) ether	<0.14
Bis(2-ethylhexyl) phthalate	<7.2
Bromodichloromethane	<0.1
Chlorobenzene	<0.1
Chrysene, water	**E 0.08**
cis-1,2-Dichloroethene	<0.1
Dibenzo[a,h]anthracene	<0.42
Dibromochloromethane	<0.2
Dichlorodifluoromethane	<0.2
Dichloromethane	<0.2
Diethyl ether	<0.2

Table 13. Volatile and semivolatile organic compounds in a single stormwater grab sample taken within the first 30 minutes of runoff from heating and cooling station SWR11–4, Fort Gordon, Georgia, August 28, 2012.–Continued

[All units in micrograms per liter; <, less than; E, estimated; NR, not reported; Bold text indicates compound detected.]

Compound	Result
Diethyl phthalate	**E 0.15**
Diisopropyl ether	<0.2
Dimethyl phthalate	**E 0.02**
Di-n-butyl phthalate	**E 0.27**
Di-n-octyl phthalate	<0.6
Ethylbenzene	<0.1
Fluoranthene	**E 0.14**
Hexachlorobutadiene	<0.24
Hexachlorocyclopentadiene	<0.5
Hexachloroethane	<0.24
Indeno[1,2,3-cd]pyrene	**E 0.06**
Isophorone	**E 0.14**
Methyl tert-butyl ether	<0.2
Methyl tert-pentyl ether	<0.2
m-Xylene plus p-xylene	<0.2
Naphthalene	<0.22
Nitrobenzene	<0.26
N-Nitrosodimethylamine	<0.32
N-Nitrosodi-n-propylamine	<0.4
N-Nitrosodiphenylamine	<0.48
o-Xylene	<0.1
Phenanthrene	**E 0.05**
Phenol	**E 0.06**
Pyrene	**E 0.11**
Styrene	<0.1
tert-Butyl ethyl ether	<0.1
Tetrachloroethene	<0.1
Tetrachloromethane	<0.2
Toluene, water	<0.1
trans-1,2-Dichloroethene	<0.1
Tribromomethane	<0.2
Trichloroethene	<0.1
Trichlorofluoromethane	<0.2
Trichloromethane	<0.1
Trihalomethanes	<0.6
Vinyl chloride	<0.2

Table 14. Volatile and semivolatile organic compounds in a single stormwater grab sample taken within the first 30 minutes of runoff from heating and cooling station SWR11–5, Fort Gordon, Georgia, August 28, 2012.

[All units in micrograms per liter; <, less than; E, estimated; NR, not reported; Bold text indicates compound detected.]

Compound	Result
1,2-Dichloroethane	<0.2
1,2-Dichloropropane	<0.1
1,4-Dichlorobenzene	<0.1
2,4,6-Trichlorophenol	<0.34
2,4-Dichlorophenol	<0.36
2,4-Dimethylphenol	<0.8
2-Methyl-4,6-dinitrophenol	<2
4-Chloro-3-methylphenol	<0.54
4-Nitrophenol	**E 0.25**
Hexachlorobenzene	<0.3
Pentachlorophenol	**E 0.1**
1,1,1-Trichloroethane	<0.1
1,1,2-Trichloro-1,2,2-trifluoroethane	<0.1
1,1-Dichloroethane	<0.1
1,1-Dichloroethene	<0.1
1,2,4-Trichlorobenzene	<0.26
1,2-Dichlorobenzene	<0.1
1,2-Diphenylhydrazine	<0.3
1,3-Dichlorobenzene	<0.1
2,4-Dinitrophenol	<2
2,4-Dinitrotoluene	<0.56
2,6-Dinitrotoluene	<0.4
2-Chloronaphthalene	<0.24
2-Nitrophenol	<0.4
3,3'-Dichlorobenzidine	<0.42
4-Bromophenyl phenyl ether	<0.24
4-Chlorophenyl phenyl ether	<0.34
9H-Fluorene, water	**0.04**
Acenaphthene	<0.28
Acenaphthylene	<0.3
Anthracene, water	**0.06**
Benzene, water	<0.1
Benzo[*a*]anthracene	**0.11**
Benzo[*a*]pyrene	**0.34**
Benzo[*b*]fluoranthene	**E 0.76**
Benzo[*ghi*]perylene	**0.4**
Benzo[*k*]fluoranthene	**E 0.38**
Benzyl n-butyl phthalate	**E 0.4**
Bis(2-chloroethoxy)methane	<0.24
Bis(2-chloroethyl) ether	<0.3
Bis(2-chloroisopropyl) ether	<0.14
Bis(2-ethylhexyl) phthalate	<7.2
Bromodichloromethane	<0.1
Chlorobenzene	<0.1
Chrysene, water	**0.71**
cis-1,2-Dichloroethene	<0.1
Dibenzo[*a,h*]anthracene	<0.42
Dibromochloromethane	<0.2
Dichlorodifluoromethane	<0.2
Dichloromethane	<0.2
Diethyl ether	<0.2

Table 14. Volatile and semivolatile organic compounds in a single stormwater grab sample taken within the first 30 minutes of runoff from heating and cooling station SWR11–5, Fort Gordon, Georgia, August 28, 2012.–Continued

[All units in micrograms per liter; <, less than; E, estimated; NR, not reported; Bold text indicates compound detected.]

Compound	Result
Diethyl phthalate	**0.31**
Diisopropyl ether	<0.2
Dimethyl phthalate	**0.03**
Di-n-butyl phthalate	**E 0.21**
Di-n-octyl phthalate	**E 0.6**
Ethylbenzene	<0.1
Fluoranthene	<1.24
Hexachlorobutadiene	<0.24
Hexachlorocyclopentadiene	<0.5
Hexachloroethane	<0.24
Indeno[1,2,3-*cd*]pyrene	**E 0.34**
Isophorone	**E 0.34**
Methyl tert-butyl ether	<0.2
Methyl tert-pentyl ether	<0.2
m-Xylene plus p-xylene	<0.2
Naphthalene	<0.04
Nitrobenzene	<0.26
N-Nitrosodimethylamine	<0.32
N-Nitrosodi-n-propylamine	<0.4
N-Nitrosodiphenylamine	<0.48
o-Xylene	<0.1
Phenanthrene	**0.51**
Phenol	**0.39**
Pyrene	**0.86**
Styrene	<0.1
tert-Butyl ethyl ether	<0.1
Tetrachloroethene	<0.1
Tetrachloromethane	<0.2
Toluene, water	<0.1
trans-1,2-Dichloroethene	<0.1
Tribromomethane	<0.2
Trichloroethene	<0.1
Trichlorofluoromethane	<0.2
Trichloromethane	<0.1
Trihalomethanes	<0.6
Vinyl chloride	<0.2

Table 15. Detected semivolatile organic compounds in a single stormwater grab sample taken within the first 30 minutes of runoff from heating and cooling stations, Fort Gordon, Georgia, August 28, 2012.

[All units in micrograms per liter; <, less than; E, estimated; M, values that are detected at a level below method detection limits but unable to be quantified; NR, not reported; Bold text indicates compound detected.]

Compound	SWR11–3	SWR11–4	SWR11–5
Polycyclic Aromatic Hydrocarbons			
9H-Fluorene, water	<0.34	<0.34	**0.04**
Anthracene, water	<0.38	<0.38	**0.06**
Benzo[a]anthracene	**0.04**	<0.26	**0.11**
Benzo[a]pyrene	**0.08**	**0.06**	**0.34**
Benzo[b]fluoranthene	**E 0.15**	**E 0.12**	**E 0.76**
Benzo[ghi]perylene	**0.07**	**E 0.07**	**0.4**
Benzo[k]fluoranthene	**E 0.08**	**E 0.05**	**E 0.38**
Chrysene, water	**0.12**	**E 0.08**	**0.71**
Fluoranthene	**0.15**	**E 0.14**	<1.24
Indeno[1,2,3-cd]pyrene	**E 0.06**	**E 0.06**	**E 0.34**
Naphthalene	**0.03**	<0.22	< 0.04
Phenanthrene	**0.04**	**E 0.05**	**0.51**
Pyrene	**0.12**	**E 0.11**	**0.86**
Total PAH concentration	**0.94**	**0.74**	**4.51**

Compound	SWR11–3	SWR11–4	SWR11–5
Other Semivolatile Organic Compounds			
4-Nitrophenol	<0.52	<0.52	**E 0.25**
Pentachlorophenol	**E 0.1**	**M**	**E 0.1**
Diethyl phthalate	<0.62	**E 0.15**	**0.31**
Dimethyl phthalate	**0.03**	**E 0.02**	**0.03**
Di-n-butyl phthalate	<2.8	**E 0.27**	**E 0.21**
Di-n-octyl phthalate	<0.6	<0.6	**E 0.6**
Benzyl n-butyl phthalate	**E 0.6**	<1.8	**E 0.4**
Isophorone	**E 0.23**	**E 0.14**	**E 0.34**
Phenol	**0.12**	**E 0.06**	**0.39**
Total Detected Compounds	**16**	**15**	**20**

Summary

The U.S. Geological Survey, in cooperation with the U.S. Department of the Army Environmental and Natural Resources Management Office of the U.S. Army Signal Center and Fort Gordon, assessed the quantity and quality of stormwater runoff associated with industrial activities from January through August 2012. The assessment was conducted to satisfy the requirements from a general permit that authorizes the discharge of stormwater under the National Pollutant Discharge Elimination System from a site with industrial activities.

Stormwater runoff was sampled from five stations at four industrial sites (two landfills, sites SWR11–1 and SWR11–2, and three heating and cooling sites, SWR11–3, SWR11–4, and SWR11–5). The assessment included the collection rainfall amounts, discharges, and field parameters (water temperature, specific conductance, dissolved oxygen, and pH); the detection of suspended materials (total suspended solids, total fixed solids, total volatile solids), nutrients and organic compounds, and major and trace inorganic compounds; and the detection of volatile and semivolatile organic compounds (heating and cooling sites only). The largest rainfall amount was of 1.0 inch at station SWR11–2. The results for all five samples indicate that many of the constituents were detected above their laboratory reporting levels.

Landfill site SWR11–2 had the largest total suspended solids concentration (214 milligrams per liter, mg/L) with most of the suspended solids consisting of fixed solids (176 mg/L) rather than volatile solids (38 mg/L). The total suspended solids concentration at site SWR11–2 exceeded the maximum daily effluent limit for total suspended solids of 88 mg/L. Heating and cooling site SWR11–3 had the highest concentrations of total suspended solids (169 mg/L), total fixed solids (101 mg/L), and total volatile solids (68 mg/L) when compared to other two heating and cooling sites. Total nitrogen and phosphorus concentrations were 1.02 and 0.09, and 1.74 and 0.21 mg/L, respectively at landfill sites SWR11–1 and SWR11–2. Heating and cooling sites total nitrogen and total phosphorus concentrations ranged from 0.53 to 1.08 mg/L and 0.07 to 0.1 mg/L, respectively, with the highest concentrations measured at site SWR11–3. Chemical oxygen demand was measured at 18 and 19.6 mg/L at landfill sites SWR11–1 and SWR11–2, respectively, which are less than the maximum daily effluent limit for 5-day BOD (140 mg/L). Chemical oxygen demand ranged from 20 to 60 mg/L for the heating and cooling sites. The largest COD (60 mg/L) was measured at site SWR11–3. Additionally, oil and grease concentrations at the heating and cooling sites were compared to applicable benchmark standards; no sample concentrations exceeded these standards.

The estimated dissolved concentrations of cadmium, lead, nickel, zinc, mercury, and silver, and the total recoverable concentrations of arsenic and selenium were compared to applicable benchmark, acute and chronic effect criteria. The estimated dissolved zinc concentration (105 micrograms per liter) at site SWR11–3 was the only constituent to exceed a benchmark standard (40 micrograms per liter). Estimated dissolved zinc concentrations at sites SWR11–4 and SWR11–5 exceeded acute and chronic effect aquatic-life criteria. Estimated dissolved concentrations of lead exceeded the chronic effect aquatic-life criteria at all sites and exceeded the acute effect aquatic-life criteria at site SWR11–3. The acute and chronic effect aquatic-life criteria for dissolved cadmium were exceeded at site SWR11–3.

Samples from sites SWR11–3, SWR11–4, and SWR11–5 were analyzed for 83 volatile and semivolatile organic compounds. Eight polycyclic aromatic hydrocarbon compounds, benzo[*a*]pyrene, benzo[*b*]fluoranthene, benzo[ghi]perylene, benzo[*k*]fluoranthene, chrysene, indeno[1,2,3-*cd*]pyrene, phenanthrene, and pyrene, were detected at all three sites. Other semivolatile organic compounds detected at all three sites included pentachlorophenol, dimethyl phthalate, and isophorone. Of the 83 volatile and semivolatile organic compounds that were analyzed in stormwater samples from heating and cooling sites, 15 (18 percent) were detected at site SWR11–3, 12 (14 percent) were detected at site SWR11–4, and 17 (20 percent) were detected at site SWR11–5.

References Cited

Bohdaine, G.L., 1968, Measurement of peak discharge at culverts by indirect methods: U.S. Geological Survey Techniques of Water-Resources Investigations, book 3, chap. A3, 60 p.

Childress, C.J.O., Foreman, W.T., Connor, B.F., Maloney, T.J., 1999, New reporting procedures based on long-term method detection levels and some considerations for interpretations of water-quality data provided by the U. S. Geological Survey National Water Quality Laboratory: U.S. Geological Survey Open-File Report 99–193, 19 p.

Church, P.E., Granato, G.E., and Owens, D.W., 1999, Basic requirements for collecting, documenting, and reporting precipitation and storm-flow measurements: U.S. Geological Survey Open-File Report 99–255, 38 p.

Connor, B.F., Rose, D.L., Noriega, M.C., Murtagh, L., Abney, S.R., 1997, Methods of analysis by the U.S. Geological Survey water quality laboratories—Determination of 86 volatile organic compounds in water by gas spectrometry, including detections less than reporting limits., U.S. Geological Survey Open-File Report 97–829, 78 p.

Fishman, M.J, ed., 1993, Methods of analysis by the U.S. Geological Survey National Water Quality Laboratory—Determination of inorganic constituents in water and fluvial sediments: U.S. Geological Survey Open-File Report 93–125, 217 p.

Fishman, M.J., and Friedman, L.C., 1989, Methods for determination of inorganic substances in water and fluvial sediments: U.S. Geological Survey Techniques of Water-Resources Investigations, book 5, chapter A1, 545 p.

Garbarino, J.R., and Damrau, D.L., 2001, Methods of analysis by the U.S. Geological Survey National Water Quality Laboratory—Determination of organic plus inorganic in filtered and unfiltered natural waters with cold vapor—Atomic fluorescence spectrometry: U.S. Geological Survey Water-Resources Investigations Report 01–4132, 16 p.

Garbarino, J.R., Kanagt, L.K., and Cree, M.E., 2006, Determination of elements in natural water, biota, sediment, and soil samples using collision/reaction cell inductively coupled plasma-mass spectrometry: U.S. Geological Survey Techniques and Methods, book 5, sec. B, chap. 1, 88 p.

Garbarino, J.R., and Struzeski, T.M., 1998, Methods of analysis by the U.S. Geological Survey National Water Quality Laboratory—Determination of elements in whole-water digests using inductively coupled plasma-optical emissions spectrometry and inductively coupled plasma-mass spectrometry: U.S. Geological Survey Open-File Report 98–165, 101 p.

Georgia Department of Natural Resources, 2006, Authorization to discharge under the National Pollutant Discharge Elimination System—Storm Water Discharges associated with Industrial Activity , General Permit No.GAR000000, effective date August 1, 2006, through July 31, 2011, accessed on March 21, 2013, at *http://www.gaepd.org/ Files_PDF/techguide/wpb/Industrial_SW_General_ Permit_GAR000000_Y2006_June8.pdf*

Georgia Department of Natural Resources, 2012a, Authorization to discharge under the National Pollutant Discharge Elimination System—Storm water discharges associated with industrial activities, general NPDES stormwater permit No. GAR050000, effective date June 1, 2012, through May 31, 2017, accessed March 28, 2012, at *http://www.gaepd.org/Documents/techguide_wpb.html.*

Georgia Department of Natural Resources, 2012b, Water use classifications and water quality standards—Code of Federal Registry 391-3-6-.03, accessed 1/10/2013, at *http://www.gaepd.org/Files_PDF/techguide/wpb/WQS/ EPA_Approved_WQS_March2012.pdf.*

Gregory, M.B., Stamey, T.C., and Wellborn, J.B., 2001, Eco¬logical characterization of streams, and fish-tissue analysis for mercury and lead at selected locations, Fort Gordon, Georgia, June 1999 to May 2000: U.S. Geological Survey Open-File Report 01–203, 14 p.

Hoffman, G.L., Fishman, M.J., and Garbarino, J.R., 1996, Methods of analysis by the U.S. Geological Survey National Water Quality Laboratory—In bottle acid digestion of whole-water samples: U.S. Geological Survey Open-File Report 96–225, 28 p.

National Water Quality Laboratory method holding times 2010: Accessed April 25, 2013, at *http://nwql.usgs.gov/Public/pubs/Method%20holding%20 times%205-25-10.pdf.*

O'Dell, J.W., 1993, Method 350.1 – determination of ammonia nitrogen by semi-automated colorimetry, Revision 2.0: U.S. Environmental Protection Agency, Office of Research and Development, accessed 06/05/2013 at *http://water.epa.gov/ scitech/methods/cwa/bioindicators/upload/2007_07_10_ methods_method_350_1.pdf.*

Patton, C.J., and Kryskalla, J.R., 2003, Methods of analysis by the U.S. Geological Survey National Water Pollution Laboratory—Evaluation of alkaline persulfate digestion as an alternative to Kjeldhal digestion for determination of total and dissolved nitrogen and phosphorus in water: U.S. Geological Survey Open-File Report 03–4174, 33 p.

Standard methods for the examination of water and wastewater, 21st edition, 2005, Method 5310B high temperature combustion method: Accessed April 7, 2012, at *http://www.standardmethods.org/store/ProductView. cfm?ProductID=38.*

Teledyne Isco, Inc., 2007, 750 Area velocity module installation and operation guide: Teledyne Isco, Inc., 39 p.

Teledyne Isco, Inc., 2012, 6712 Portable samplers installation and operation guide: Teledyne Isco, Inc., 246 p.

U.S. Environmental Protection Agency, 1992, National pollutant discharge elimination system storm water sampling guidance document: Washington, D.C., Office of Water, Report EPA 883-B-92-001, 177 p.

U.S. Environmental Protection Agency, 1999a, Analytical methods-method 1664, revision A; n-hexane extractable material (HEM; oil and grease) and silica gel treated n-hexane extractable material (SGT-HEM; non-polar material) by extraction and gravimetry: Report EPA 821-R-98-002, 23 p.

U.S. Environmental Protection Agency, 1999b, USEPA Contract laboratory program national functional guidelines for organic data review: Office of Emergency and Remedial Response, Washington, D.C., Report EPA 540-R-99-008, 118 p.

U.S. Environmental Protection Agency, 2004, USEPA Contract laboratory program national functional guidelines for inorganic data review: Washington, D.C., Office of Emergency and Remedial Response, EPA 540-R-04-004, 136 p.

U. S. Environmental Protection Agency, 2006, National Recommended Water Quality Criteria: U. S. Environmental Protection Agency Office of Water (4304T), accessed June 05, 2013, at *http://nepis.epa.gov/Exe/ZyNET.exe/P1003R9X. TXT?ZyActionD=ZyDocument&Client=EPA&Index=2006 +Thru+2010&Docs=&Query=&Time=&EndTime=&Searc hMethod=1&TocRestrict=n&Toc=&TocEntry=&QField=& QFieldYear=&QFieldMonth=&QFieldDay=&IntQFieldO p=0&ExtQFieldOp=0&XmlQuery=&File=D%3A%5Czyfil es%5CIndex%20Data%5C06thru10%5CTxt%5C00000007 %5CP1003R9X.txt&User=ANONYMOUS&Password=ano nymous&SortMethod=h%7C-&MaximumDocuments=1&F uzzyDegree=0&ImageQuality=r75g8/r75g8/x150y150g16/ i425&Display=p%7Cf&DefSeekPage=x&SearchBack=ZyA ctionL&Back=ZyActionS&BackDesc=Results%20page&M aximumPages=1&ZyEntry=1&SeekPage=x&ZyPURL*

U.S. Environmental Protection Agency, 2009, Industrial stormwater monitoring and sampling guide: U.S. Environmental Protection Agency Report, EPA 832-B-09-003, 51p.

U.S. Geological Survey, 2012, National Water Quality Laboratory—Quality: Accessed 06/06/2013 at *http://nwql.usgs.gov/quality.shtml.*

U.S. Geological Survey, variously dated, National field manual for the collection of water-quality data: U.S. Geological Survey Techniques of Water-Resources Investigations, book 9, chaps. A1–A9, accessed March 26, 2012, at *http://pubs.water.usgs.gov/twri9A.*